Buff Orpingtons: The Complete Owner's Guide

The Must Have Guide for Anyone Passionate About Owning, Breeding or Showing Buff Orpington Chickens

By Ruth L. Corbin

ISBN 978-0-9985655-1-4

Heath Publishing Company
1525 Carlos Dr.
Greenville, NC 27834

Table of Contents

Introduction

Whether you already own Buff Orpingtons or you are considering owning them, this is the book for you. This is not a book on general chicken care, which is well covered by other sources. After reading this book you will be an expert on Buff Orpington chickens. You will be able to:

- Describe the history of the Buff Orpington breed in stunning detail
- Know what characteristics and traits to expect from your Buff Orpingtons
- Optimize housing and feeding for your Buff Orpingtons
- Selectively breed Buff Orpingtons to produce your own prize winning show birds
- Safely keep Buff Orpingtons as family pets
- Use your Buff Orpingtons for fresh eggs and meat
- Hatch Buff Orpington eggs both naturally and through incubation
- Determine whether your local climate is suitable for Buff Orpingtons
- Identify vitamin deficiency by a key sign unique to Buff Orpingtons
- Weigh the pros and cons of the Buff Orpington breed
- Make an educated decision on whether Buff Orpingtons are the breed for you
- Provide customized, expert care for your Buff Orpington chickens

I know you are excited to get started, so let's jump right into it!

Chapter 1: History of Buff Orpingtons

Orpington chickens were developed by William Cook (pictured above) in Kent County, Orpington, England in 1886. Cook was born in the town of St. Neots in Cambridgeshire County, England in 1849. He did not come from a poultry raising family, but developed his own interest in poultry in his teenage years.

At the age of 20 he moved to Orpington, England with his wife Jane. After experimenting with many breeds of chickens, Cook found that none of these completely met his purposes. That was the moment Cook decided to create his own breed. Cook's goal was to develop a cold hardy, fast growing, general utility chicken (laid well and had good meat). He created the first Orpington chickens (the single comb Black Orpington) by cross-breeding Minorca roosters with Black Plymouth Rock hens. He then cross-bred the Minorca/Black Plymouth hybrid chickens with Langshan chickens.

The Buff Orpington is the gold or buff color variety of the Orpington chicken. Cook developed the Buff Orpington by cross breeding Golden Spangled Hamburg roosters with Buff Cochin hens. Then he cross-bred the Golden Spangled Hamburg/Buff Cochin hybrid hens with dark or colored Dorking roosters. Finally, he cross-bred that hybrid offspring back with Buff Cochin hens (Figure 1).

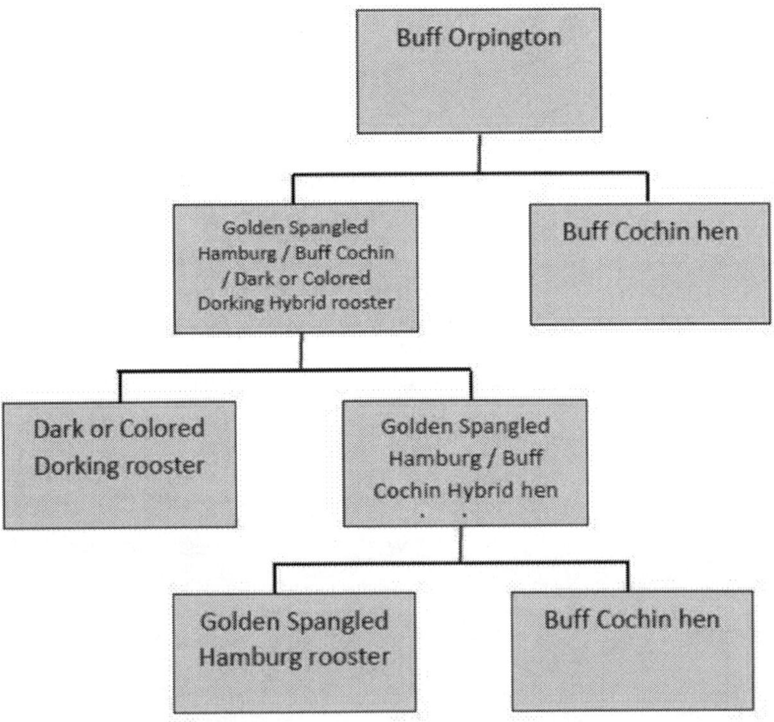

Figure 1: Cook's process for developing the Buff Orpington breed.

Cook was exceedingly proud of the Buff Orpington breed he created. He introduced the Buff Orpington in England in 1894. Then the trouble began. There were claims that someone else had developed the Buff Orpington breed first, but under a different name. The Orpington Club in England protested strongly against Cook's Buff Orpingtons being classified as Orpington chickens.

The Orpington Club and other critics of Cook's Buff Orpingtons claimed that there had already been a similar breed developed Lincoln County, England twenty years earlier. This breed was known as the Lincolnshire Buff. The Orpington Club and many Lincolnshire Buff breeders claimed that although some of the chickens being referred to as Buff Orpingtons were produced in Kent by William Cook, the majority of chickens being referred to as Buff Orpingtons were directly bred from Lincolnshire Buffs, without the slightest relationship to Cook's strain. They claimed that Cook copied the Lincolnshire Buff breed very closely, while making minor changes for uniformity and standardization in the Buff Orpington breed. You can compare the relationship for yourself.

The Lincolnshire Buff breed was originally developed by cross-breeding Dorkings and Common Fowls, then cross-breeding the Dorking/Common Fowl hybrid hens with Buff Cochin roosters. So, the Dorking and Buff Cochin are present in both the Buff Orpington and the Lincolnshire Buff. The difference is that Buff Orpingtons also were cross-bred with Golden Spangled Hamburgs. You may recall that the original Black Orpingtons were developed by cross-breeding Minorca roosters with Black Plymouth Rock hens, followed by cross-breeding the

Minorca/Black Plymouth hybrid chickens with Langshan chickens. None of these breeds were present in the Buff Orpington.

You can see that Buff Orpingtons are more closely related to Lincolnshire Buffs than other Orpington chickens. But the question of the day was whether their differences would be enough to sustain Cook's breed. Cook insisted on the superiority and differences of the Buff Orpington breed. While the legs of the Lincolnshire Buff were feathered, the Buff Orpingtons legs were clean. The Buff Orpington had four toes while the Lincolnshire Buff had five. The Buff Orpington had a shorter back than the Lincolnshire Buff, carried its tail higher, and had fluffier feathering. Because the Buff Orpingtons were smaller, they also required less room. Still, the Orpington Club and many Lincolnshire Buff breeders agreed that the Buff Orpington breed was too similar to the Lincolnshire Buff to be its own breed.

Cook was a writer on poultry topics at the time, and had a lot of inside connections in publishing circles, including the English Poultry Press. He ran major advertising campaigns saying how the Buff Orpington was the best all-around chicken; excellent meat for roasting, good egg layer (including during winter months), friendly temperament, perfect size for small lot owners, cold-hardy, and a beautiful show bird. These advertisements may have had some part in consumers' preference for Buff Orpingtons above Lincolnshire Buffs. Some referred to Cook as an exploiter rather than an originator.

Cook was the triumphant party in this disagreement. The English Poultry Club declared the Single Comb and Rose Comb Buff Orpingtons as Standard Breeds in 1901. The Single Comb

Buff Orpington was admitted to the Standard of Perfection by the English Poultry Club in 1904. Breeders were able to get two to three times as much money for Buff Orpingtons as compared to Lincolnshire Buffs, so many breeders simply changed the name they were using. By 1920, the Lincolnshire Buff name had died out. They had been replaced by the Buff Orpingtons. (However, the name was brought back in the 1980s, and Lincolnshire Buffs were officially declared a Standard Breed in 1997 by the Great Britain Poultry Club, almost 150 years after the breed's original creation.)

The Buff Orpington chickens made their way to the United States shortly after they were developed In England, although it took American breeders some time to become fond of them. The American market favored yellow-skinned and yellow-legged chickens. The pink legs and white skin of the Buff Orpington were a market handicap in the United States.

When Buff Orpingtons were first exhibited in the United States at the Madison Square Garden Show in New York in 1899, there were only twelve single chickens and one pen of Buff Orpingtons entered. In the 1901 show there were only nineteen single entries and one pen. The American Poultry Association (APA) recognized the Buff Orpington as a Standard Breed in 1902.

With the endorsement from the APA, the desirable qualities of the Buff Orpington won out, and their popularity soared in the United States and Canada over the next few years. When William Cook died in 1904, Buff Orpingtons and other Orpington varieties were the most popular breeds in England,

and they were very popular in the United States and Canada as well. The Buff Orpington was and still is the most popular Orpington variety in the United States. By the 1909 Madison Square Garden show there were 157 Buff Orpingtons entered!

Of the most popular general utility breeds in the early 20th century U.S. (the Plymouth Rocks, Rhode Island Reds, Wyandottes, and the Buff Orpingtons) the Buff Orpington was the only breed developed outside the country. Buff Orpingtons were most in favor with amateurs and those with small lots that wanted a good backyard flock. Professional farmers tended to stick with the breeds that they had success with for years, and they paid less attention to the advertisements claiming that the Orpingtons were easily three times more profitable than other breeds. They were unwilling to pay the high prices for Orpington chicks and eggs, which cut into their profits since they had to buy in large quantities. Buff Orpingtons were also popular among professional showmen because they had beautiful soft golden plumage, did not show dirt as much as other breeds, and had no dark pin feathers (objectionable when considering show qualities).

The fact that Buff Orpingtons were most popular amongst families and other small plot holders as backyard flocks contributed to their decline. The poultry business became dominated by a handful of large corporations with the industrialization of the 20th century. Many small family farmers shut down their farms and moved to the cities In search of work.

"PERTELOTE"
First Prize Hen New York, 1908. Owned by Miss Henrietta E. Hooker.

The Buff Orpington was categorized as endangered by the Rare Breeds Survival Trust in England when the organization was founded in 1973. The Buff Orpington was categorized as threatened by the Livestock Conservancy when they were founded in 1977 (at that time the group was called the American Minor Breeds Conservancy). The genetic variety of poultry breeds was at risk as the Buff Orpington and other classic breeds our ancestors developed were being forgotten and specialized commercial breeds were becoming the norm for consumption.

Backyard chickens have become popular again in recent times. People like you have brought back the tradition of families keeping chickens. Your reason might be that you have become concerned with the treatment and living conditions of factory farmed chickens and have also become concerned with chemicals and antibiotics in food production. You may want to raise chickens for meat and/or eggs to ease your grocery budget. You might just want to keep chickens as pets and the fresh eggs are a bonus. You may want to show your children where food comes from.

No matter what your reason is, endangered breeds of chickens are recovering because of this trend that you are a part of. The Livestock Conservancy and the Rare Breeds Survival Trust promote heritage breeds such as the Buff Orpington for backyard flocks. The groups emphasize the need for genetic diversity in poultry (the less diversity, the higher the risk of a disease wiping out much of the poultry in the country).

The Buff Orpington's population numbers have recently recovered. This is due to the breed's recent popularity amongst backyard flock owners like you in the United States, Canada, England, and Australia. In their most recent Priority Poultry list released in 2016, the Livestock Conservancy graduated the Buff Orpington and other Orpington breeds (meaning they are no longer on the list). However, the Buff Orpington remains on the watch list for the Rare Breeds Survival Trust (although they no longer list the breed as endangered).

Chapter 2: Characteristics & Traits of Buff Orpingtons

Source= [http://www.flickr.com/photos/26454069@N03/2771672568/ Battle chicken is ready for action] |Date=August 17, 2008 at 11:11 |Author=[http://www.flickr.com/people/264540]

Buff Orpingtons are one of the friendliest breeds of chickens you can get. Buff Orpingtons usually make good family pets and are a great choice for a backyard flock. You will enjoy seeing these beautiful birds in your yard.

The beauty of the buff color is appreciated by most, and the breed is popular for use as show birds. They also have a very mild temperament compared to other breeds. They generally have a calm, friendly disposition. They are easy to raise compared to other breeds. Even the roosters are generally docile, although this is not always the case. I have seen aggressive roosters in this breed, but not nearly as often as with other breeds. I have never seen an aggressive Buff Orpington hen. The hens from our flock of Buff Orpingtons were very sweet, you could even pick them up and pet them.

The buff (golden) plumage of the Buff Orpington is soft to the touch. Their under-layer of feathers is a lighter shade of buff. Buff Orpingtons have white skin. Their combs, faces, wattles (hangs from neck) and earlobes are red. They have a light pink beak and usually have red eyes. Their shape is round, broad and deep. Buff Orpingtons have short legs so their bodies sit low to the ground. They are heavily and loosely feathered, although not as loose as some other breeds such as the Cochin.

Buff Orpingtons are known for having tender and delicious meat, being prolific year-round layers, and being very winter hardy. While you can find breeds that lay more eggs, or grow more quickly for meat production, the Buff Orpington is one of the best all-purpose breeds you can get.

Buff Orpingtons are relatively large chickens. The roosters weigh between 9 – 10 pounds while the hens weigh between 7 – 8 pounds when they are mature. Their large size is part of the reason they are adapted to snowy weather. If you live in a northern area with cold winters, the Buff Orpington is a good choice. They stand the cold very well and will keep laying eggs all winter. Many breeds of chickens are not so adapted to the cold, especially smaller breeds.

Buff Orpingtons are active birds, and while they don't require a great deal of space, if you give them a bit of freedom to roam around they will be happier and will supplement their feeding by eating worms and other insects along with natural plant matter. They are naturally great foragers. This not only saves you money on chicken feed, but makes the eggs and meat taste much richer.

However, if space is an issue, never fear. Buff Orpingtons do also make great city birds. Just be sure to check your local ordinances if you live in a city or town limits. Rules are determined locally and differ from city to city. Many cities are allowing people to have a certain number of laying hens, while some are not. Very few cities allow roosters. Your best bet would be to speak to someone in the Planning or Zoning Department at your City Hall. If you live in the county (or other equivalent outside the city limits), this should not be an issue for you.

The Buff Orpington is a great breed for all purposes, whether to enter in shows, use for eggs and meat, or to have as family pets. Many people say Buff Orpingtons are the best chickens they have ever raised. While they are a popular breed for amateurs because of their easy going temperament, they are also well praised by people who have experience with a variety of poultry breeds. After having backyard flocks consisting a variety of breeds, many experienced chicken owners agree that the Buff Orpington is the best breed of all.

Chapter 3: Housing and Feeding Buff Orpingtons

Source: https://commons.wikimedia.org/wiki/File:Buff-orpington-rooster.jpg, English: Buff Orpington Rooster Date 15 March 2011 Source Own work Author OKFarmgirl

As with any breed, Buff Orpingtons will need a chicken coop to lay eggs in, sleep in, and protect them from predators. They will also need a fence to contain them if you want to let them out of the coop (recommended if possible).

I won't go into detail on how to construct a chicken coop, but I will discuss what is unique about housing Buff Orpingtons as compared to other breeds. First, here are some resources in case you don't have a chicken coop yet.

You can build a chicken coop yourself and save a ton of money if you have basic carpentry skills. However, working out dimensions, materials, insulation, ventilation, lighting, positioning, nesting, perches, waste collection and protection from the elements and predators can seem complicated. Fortunately, you can get an easy to follow guide to building your own chicken coop. You get multiple blueprints in the guide so you can customize the coop to your size and budget needs. You also get supply lists and detailed instructions so you know exactly what to buy and what steps to take. This guide has helped thousands of people build their own affordable backyard chicken coops. You can do the same by getting your guide at http://bufforpingtons.net/coopguide.

If you don't feel comfortable building a chicken coop from scratch, I would recommend http://bufforpingtons.net/chickencoops. These are the Rolls Royce's of chicken coops. They are high quality, durable, oversized coops that literally require no effort on your part. Your chickens will practically have a house. You could keep chickens your whole life and never need another coop. Beware of very cheap chicken coops that you screw together like pressboard furniture. These will not hold up over time and offer no insulation for your chickens if you live in a cold climate.

Now, let's discuss what is unique about housing Buff Orpingtons. Buff Orpingtons are very laid back and docile compared with other breeds. If your Buff Orpingtons are housed with more aggressive breeds they may be attacked by the others, who will tend to take their kindness as a weakness. If you do plan to have a mixed flock, observe the behavior of the chickens to make sure your Buff Orpingtons are not being bullied.

Because they are so easy going, Buff Orpingtons are less likely to try to escape than other breeds. Usually they are too fat and heavy to fly over a fence of decent height anyway. Because of their large size, it is a good idea to go with larger sized nesting boxes in the chicken coop. If you are limited on space Bantam Buff Orpingtons are a good choice. They are basically a miniature version of the breed and display the same docile temperament. Bantam Buff Orpingtons make great pets. Just note that if you are using them for eggs, Bantam eggs have a higher yolk to egg white content.

Because Buff Orpingtons are large birds that are heavily and loosely feathered, they do well in cold climates. If you live up north where there is snow most of the winter this is a consideration. If you live in a tropical or desert area this is also a consideration, as the Buff Orpingtons may feel hot in that climate. Smaller breeds tend to fare better in very hot climates.

Feeding Buff Orpingtons is like feeding any other chickens, although they do have some unique qualities. The Buff Orpington is a slow growing breed. Therefore, they can benefit from being on starter feed longer than most breeds. While most breeds need starter chick feed (20 – 22 percent protein) until about six weeks of age, Buff Orpingtons should receive starter feed for about eight weeks.

Most breeds would then be fed a pullet grower feed (14 – 16 percent protein) until about age 20 weeks, but Buff Orpingtons should receive pullet grower feed until about 24 weeks of age. Then you can start feeding them layer feed (15-18 percent protein). You can mix cracked corn in with the layer feed. This is especially a good idea during cold winter months. If you were raising your Buff Orpingtons for meat, you would switch right to a broiler finisher feed from the starter chick feed at eight weeks. You would not need the pullet grower feed.

Most people buy pre-mixed chicken feed. You can get this at any agricultural supply store. You can mix your own chicken feed if you desire and have the time. You might want to if you are raising Buff Orpingtons as show birds. As with people they are healthier and more beautiful if they have a good diet. A very strict time tested method is feeding chick starter feed with hard-boiled egg chopped fine for the first three weeks, then adding rolled oats to the mixture until they are eight weeks old. After they are eight weeks old they are fed a mash made of coarse cornmeal and rolled oatmeal soaked overnight in skim milk in the morning, midday they are given boiled potatoes, carrots and beets, and for dinner they are given whole wheat. Wheat bran can be available at all times, but never give more of the other rations than they can eat up clean. Do not feed corn to show birds except on cold winter nights. If the birds are able to have free range, natural bugs and forage will also be beneficial.

Adding any of these natural food sources will be good for your Buff Orpingtons and they will appreciate it too. It does not have to be all store bought feed or all fresh food, it can be a combination. Most people provide store bought feed as the staple, and supplement with fresh food. If Buff Orpingtons are allowed free range at least part time and/or are given fresh vegetables and grains, they will have richer eggs and tastier meat. There is also a difference in quality between brands of store bought feed. Be sure to check the protein content and compare with the guidelines above. Read the ingredients so you know what you are feeding your chickens.

Even a small enclosure outside the chicken coop is sufficient for your Buff Orpingtons to find worms and bugs to eat.

Buff Orpingtons also do well as city birds so no problem there. If you live in the city where they will remain in the chicken coop or cages, you can still supplement by purchasing worms or fresh veggies for your chickens. Worms can be bought at any fishing tackle shop and at some pet stores.

Buff Orpingtons should not have black in their feathers. If they do, it may be a sign of Vitamin D deficiency. This shouldn't be a problem if you are using pre-mixed feed (which is fortified) and the chickens are getting sunlight, but if you do notice this issue you can supplement their diets with either cod liver oil or a multivitamin for poultry.

Chapter 4: Buff Orpingtons as Pets & Show Birds

Buff Orpingtons have a calm, friendly disposition. They are well known as one of the best breeds to keep as pets (and by many as the absolute best). If you Google Buff Orpingtons there are a ton of blogs with people going on about how great they are. If you have children and want to have backyard chickens, Buff Orpingtons are a good choice. As compared with other breeds, Buff Orpington chickens are very friendly and have laid back personalities.

However, you still need to be cautious with children and roosters until you know how that rooster will behave when he matures. I have seen aggressive Buff Orpington roosters. That is just the nature of roosters in general, they act tough to protect their hens. Although, I have seen many docile Buff Orpington roosters as well. The docile Buff Orpingtons are usually what you hear about, but aggression can still occur with any rooster regardless of breed. However, it would be rare to find an aggressive Buff Orpington hen. Then are usually very friendly, letting you pick them up and pet them. Even if they are skittish, they may run from you, but probably won't make much fuss when you pick them up.

In addition to their friendly personalities, many people like to keep Buff Orpingtons as pets because they are beautiful birds, with their soft, fluffy golden plumage and large frames. Buff Orpingtons are also popular as show birds because of their good looks. Some people enjoy showing their Buff Orpingtons at exhibitions, shows and fairs, and even win prizes for doing so.

If you are going to show Buff Orpingtons, you need high quality birds. A show quality Buff Orpington is free from feathers on the legs and does not have specks in the body feathers. The feathers should be free from shafting or mealiness. (Make sure to judge your hens in the late fall or winter, after they have fully molted.) They should have a glossy sheen look to their outer coats, which should be an even shade of deep, rich buff color. (Males have more glossy sheen than females.) The under coat should match the surface color as closely as possible, although it will be slightly lighter in shade. Feathers must be free from foreign colors, especially wing and tail feathers. Black or gray in the wings or tail of a Buff Orpington is a serious defect when considering show qualities.

The feathers should be broad and smooth fitting on the deep and massive body of the Buff Orpington. However, the appearance of great massiveness should not be achieved by developing extreme length of feathers in the plumage. The sides of the body should be comparatively straight with full but not profuse feathering.

The comb, face, wattles and earlobes should be bright red, and the eyes should have a reddish bay. The skin color should be white while the shanks, toes and beaks should be a pinkish white. Yellow beaks, shanks, feet or skin are disqualifications. This is the American Standard of Perfection set by the American Poultry Association (APA)*. The APA defines buff as a medium shade of orange-yellow color with a rich golden cast not so intense as to show a reddish cast, nor so pale as to appear lemon or light yellow.

The English Standard is set by the Poultry Club of Great Britain**. The English Standard is less picky over the feather coloring, allowing any shade of buff from lemon buff to rich buff. The English Standard does still require the feather coloring to be uniform. It is just as strict on the skin coloring, which must be white. Yellow skin is a disqualification according to both standards.

The English Standard puts less emphasis on color, but more emphasis on shape. Both standard specify ideal shape, but the English Standard puts more points towards it (points determine winners in exhibitions). There are some differences in the American Standard and the English Standard regarding shape and body type, and these differences are outlined in Figure 2 on the next page. (These are the male standards, but the female standards are very similar. The cushion on the female should be wide but almost flat, and slightly rising to the tail, sufficient to give the back a graceful appearance with an outline approaching concave.)

The size requirements are similar for the two standards, with the English Standard being a bit more lenient. The American Standard calls for ten pound roosters, eight pound hens, eight and one-half pound cockerels (adolescent roosters), and seven pound pullets (adolescent hens). The English Standard calls for nine to ten pound roosters, seven to eight pound hens, and does not specify a weight for cockerels and pullets.

*From the American Poultry Association "Standard of Perfection" 1998 edition. For full standard you may purchase this publication at http://wwwamerpoultryassn.com

**From the Poultry Club of Great Britain "British Poultry Standards" 2008 edition. For full standard you may purchase this publication at http://www.poultryclub.org

Body Part	American Standard	English Standard
Beak	Short, stout, regularly curved	Relatively short, strong, and nicely curved
Face	Clean-cut and free from coarseness	Smooth
Eyes	Large, round, prominent	Large and bold
Wattles	Medium in size, well-rounded at lower edges	Medium length, oblong and nicely rounded at the bottom
Earlobes	Medium size, oblong, smooth	Small, elongated
Head	Medium in length, broad, deep	Small and neat, fairly full over the eyes
Neck	Rather short, slightly arched, with abundant hackle	Medium length, curved, compact and with full hackle
Back	Broad, flat at shoulders, rather long, width carried well back to base of tail; rising with a slight concave sweep to tail. Saddle feathers of medium length, abundant.	Nicely curved with a somewhat short concave outline.
Tail	Moderately long, well-spread, carried at an angle of twenty-five degrees (fifteen degrees in females) above horizontal, forming no apparent angle with back where those sections join.	Rather short and compact, flowing and high, no higher than the head and by no means "squirrel tail".

Wings	Of medium size, well-folded, carried horizontally, fronts well covered by breast feathers	Small, nicely formed, and carried close to the body
Breast	Broad, deep, well-rounded and well filled in all parts	Broad, deep and well-rounded, not flat
Body	Broad, deep, moderately long, straight, extending well forward	Deep, broad, and cobby
Legs and toes	Legs set well apart, straight when viewed from front. Lower thighs large, moderately short, well feathered. Shanks moderately short, stout, smooth. Four toes on each foot, of medium length, straight, well-spread.	Legs short and strong, the thighs almost hidden by the body feathers, well set apart. Absent of leg feathering. Four toes, straight and well-spread.
Fluff/Plumage	Lower body feather not too profuse. Fluff moderately full, showing profile of hocks.	Profuse but close, not soft, loose and fluffy, as in the Cochin, or close and hard, as in the Game.

Figure 2: American Standard and English Standard on shape and body type.

Source: https://www.flickr.com/photos/24198369@N04/7212063894/, Author bigbirdClosup

Combs are also a consideration for show birds. A medium five-point comb that is evenly serrated is best according to the American Standard, while a small five or six-point comb that is evenly serrated is best according to the English Standard. A comb should not have side sprigs according to both standards. When possible, avoid a very bad comb in either sex. Always avoid side sprigs. However, do not avoid breeding an otherwise desirable show bird just because of a bad comb. Color, size and shape are all more important. If you have a couple birds to choose between with equal of these most important qualities, choose the one with the good comb.

Here are a few additional tips to keep in mind. Do not breed birds with color defects for show. Do not breed birds with shafty or mealy feathers for this purpose either. The male is more likely to influence the color and shape while the female is more likely to influence the size. Even so, the females should have even coloring and should not be more than two shades darker than the male. Mating a dark Buff Orpington of one sex with a light Buff Orpington of another sex will very rarely, if ever, produce a bird of medium shade. It will likely produce a bird with uneven coloring and/or dark specks.

Obviously, it would be difficult to find a perfect specimen. The key to breeding Buff Orpingtons as show birds is to make up for any defects in one sex in the other sex. For example, if you have a male rooster with a poor comb that is a bit too skinny, but he has excellent color and shape, choose a large hen with a good comb. Do not take a good rooster and mate him indiscriminately with a number of hens. This hit and miss method will usually produce a lot of misses. If you choose your two or three best hens to mate with him, you will be pleased with the chicks that result. If you have a large flock, you can mate up to seven or eight hens with one rooster. Just make sure you are choosing high quality hens.

You do not have to meet every Standard of Perfection to enter a Buff Orpington in an exhibition. You can still win prizes if it is one of the best looking Buff Orpingtons there. If you want to show your Buff Orpingtons, just do your best to breed them for these qualities and feed them a healthy diet. Your diligence will pay off because you will be competing with many who just use a hit and miss method of breeding. The quality of your Buff Orpingtons will be much better than theirs if you follow these methods.

Chapter 5: Buff Orpingtons for Eggs & Meat

Source: https://www.flickr.com/photos/66992990@N00/4819372920/, Author: Joanna Bourne

Buff Orpingtons are excellent utility chickens, meaning they serve the dual purpose of providing eggs and meat. While you can find some chicken breeds specialized for laying the most eggs, they will not have the quality of meat that Buff Orpingtons do.

For being a utility breed, Buff Orpingtons are prolific layers. You can count on them to lay 180-200 eggs per year. Some will lay 250 eggs per year or more during their peak laying years. Each hen should lay 5-6 eggs per week, except for the long breaks they take twice a year for molting (5-8 weeks average molt time). The eggs will be large size and light brown to dark brown in color. The yolks will be dark yellow, almost orange, and very rich. You will notice that they taste much better than store bought eggs.

Buff Orpington hens start laying around 24-26 weeks old. They will lay steadily for 3-4 years, then occasionally until not at all. They are good winter layers. Many breeds do not lay in very cold weather. Buff Orpingtons are an exception to this. As winter layers they are equal to the best. This is an important consideration if you live in a cold climate. You can get your backyard eggs from Buff Orpingtons even in the snow.

Buff Orpington hens can be broody, which means at times they will set on their eggs and try to hatch them. They will not lay additional eggs when they go broody. Even if you take their eggs, sometimes they will continue to set on an empty nest. A broody hen may snap out of it in a few days, but it may take up to three weeks (the usual time it takes to hatch chicken eggs). It is unlikely for all your hens to go broody at once, so you don't have to worry about getting no eggs for three weeks, assuming you have multiple hens. Buff Orpingtons are also louder than many other breeds when laying eggs. They will often announce it at great lengths, which can be annoying to some people.

Buff Orpingtons are excellent chickens to raise for meat. Their large size provides sufficient quantity for a large family. The meat is also good quality, tender with a fine texture. Buff Orpingtons are ready to slaughter between 24-30 weeks of age. This is longer than breeds specialized for broiler production, but that is because Buff Orpingtons are a utility breed. Make sure they are filled out in the chest before slaughtering them to get the largest quantity of meat. If you wait until after they are three years old to slaughter them, the meat will be tougher and have a stronger flavor.

If you are raising Buff Orpingtons for eggs you would feed them starter chick feed, followed by pullet grower feed, followed by layer feed. If you were raising Buff Orpingtons for meat you would feed them starter chick feed, followed by broiler finisher feed. You can also supplement your Buff Orpingtons' diets by allowing them free range and/or providing fresh vegetables and grains. See Chapter 3 for details on feeding. If you are keeping meat chickens and egg chickens in the same pen, you can still slaughter chickens that have been fed layer feed. However, the broiler feed will maximize growth, so the quantity of meat will likely be less. For this reason, you might decide to have separate pens for egg and meat chickens.

Since this book is about Buff Orpingtons specifically, there are many topics I have not covered that not only apply to Buff Orpingtons, but to all chickens. Would you know what to do if you ran into issues such as eggs with thin shells, hens pooping in their nesting boxes, or laying eggs on the ground where they get broken? If you will be using your chickens for meat, do you know how to slaughter them? If not don't worry, because you can get this information for free by going to http://bufforpingtons.net/newsletter and signing up for the free newsletter. You will become an expert on raising chickens for fresh eggs and meat and be able to solve any problem that comes your way.

Chapter 6: Breeding Buff Orpingtons

Source: https://www.flickr.com/photos/ginapina/2317426308/, Author ginapina

Breeding Buff Orpingtons is usually not difficult, because the hens make good mothers. Buff Orpington hens will set on their eggs. I mentioned already that they can be broody at times. This is a plus if you want to hatch chicks. A broody Buff Orpington hen will stick with hatching her chicks and will protect them after they are hatched. Buff Orpington hens are such good mothers, they can even be used to hatch eggs from another breed. If you have a mixed flock this can be helpful if the mother hen will not sit on her eggs.

During breeding season, you can take the Buff Orpington rooster away from the hens in the evening and feed him all the corn he will eat. (You can buy large bags of cracked corn almost anywhere that sells chicken feed.) Then put him back with the hens in the morning. This routine will help guarantee fertilized eggs, although it isn't necessary if you don't have space or don't feel up to it.

If you are breeding your Buff Orpingtons for eggs or meat, or just to keep as pets, you will not be concerned with breeding for specific characteristics. In this case a Buff Orpington rooster can mate with 7-8 hens. If you are breeding Buff Orpingtons as show birds, you will want to pick 2-3 of your best hens to mate with your best rooster. See Chapter 4 on Show Birds for more information.

Many people choose to incubate eggs themselves and raise the chicks indoors in cages until they are large enough to go outside. Although it is lovely to see Buff Orpington hens raising their chicks in mother nature's way, there is a greater rate of fatality with this method. If you incubate the eggs yourself, you can sometimes have a 100% success rate with chick survival. The incubation period will be about 21 days for Buff Orpingtons eggs.

When starting your flock, you can buy Buff Orpington hatching eggs and an incubator instead of buying chicks. Or you can buy chicks to start your flock and incubate the eggs they lay later. This is of course more work and the incubator is an investment, but it is fun and rewarding to hatch chicks this way.

If you are going to incubate your eggs, you will want to see this inexpensive guide to building a high-quality egg incubator that is guaranteed to yield a high hatching rate. You can build this incubator using cheap parts from your local hardware store. You will not have to worry about turning the eggs, the incubator you build will do this automatically. Visit http://bufforpingtons.net/incubatorguide for details. Your incubator will be just as good as the high-end versions used in professional hatcheries.

Source: https://commons.wikimedia.org/wiki/File:Buff_Orpington_rooster_at_8_weeks_old.JPG Author Dominoe3045

If you choose to purchase an incubator, check your local agricultural supply store. Most also have websites if there is not a store near you. You can spend anywhere from $50 - $800 on an incubator depending on the level of automation (whether you turn the eggs yourself) and how many eggs it holds. Commercial sized units can go much higher in price, but this is an average range of pricing for a personal homestead sized incubator. If you go toward the lower price range, plan to turn the eggs three times per day.

You will want to introduce new Buff Orpingtons into your flock at least every three generations. This will prevent problems associated with inbreeding. If you are concerned with consistency of characteristics you should go back to the same hatchery you originally bought chicks or hatching eggs from if possible.

You will want to keep young chicks in a cage with the bottom lined with bedding. If the weather is nice the cage can be kept outside on a porch. With most breeds the chicks can safely be introduced into the pen with the other chickens by 10-12 weeks of age. Make this time 12-14 weeks for Buff Orpingtons since they are a slow growing breed. You can put them outside during the day a couple weeks earlier if you have a separate fenced off area next to the main pen. This will help them get used to each other without danger to the chicks. Whether you allow the hens to hatch their eggs or incubate them yourself, watching Buff Orpington chicks grow up is certainly a pleasure. You will be surprised by how much joy these little chicks bring to your family.

Conclusion: Are Buff Orpingtons the Breed for You?

Whether or not you decide to raise Buff Orpingtons, do consider a heritage breed of chicken. Many heritage chicken breeds are still endangered due to preference for a few fast growing breeds that suit the needs of factory farms. According to the Livestock Conservancy, a heritage chicken is one that is recognized as an American Poultry Association Standard Breed and has been since prior to mid-twentieth century, is naturally mating, has a long productive outdoor lifecycle, and has a slow growth rate. These slower growing heritage chickens have better tasting eggs and meat. And by owning them you get to help an endangered species and diversify the genetic pool of chicken breeds.

That being said, the Buff Orpington is likely going to be a great breed for you. They are definitely among the friendliest breeds of chickens you can get. They are one of the best breeds you can have around children. They will provide your family with plenty of eggs, and probably enough to sell some if you have more than three or four hens (depends on how many eggs you eat of course). Should you decide to use your Buff Orpingtons for meat, they will taste better than any chicken you can buy at the store. Plus, the eggs and meat will also be healthier than what you buy at the store. Buff Orpingtons are also beautiful birds, fun to admire in the backyard, and great show birds.

However, if you fall in one of the following categories, Buff Orpingtons might not be for you. Perhaps you are mainly concerned with egg production and making an income selling those eggs. You would not want a utility breed, you would want a breed that lays the maximum number of eggs, such as the Leghorn. If your prime objective is raising chickens for meat, you might prefer a faster growing breed for broiler production such as a Cornish breed. If you live in a very hot climate (i.e. tropical or desert), you may want to consider a smaller breed such as the Rhode Island Red or the Buff Minorca. This chart from the Livestock Conservancy can help if you are still trying to make a decision: https://livestockconservancy.org/images/uploads/docs/pickachicken.pdf.

If the desire for specialization in egg or meat production and the climatic issue do not present a problem, the Buff Orpington is going to be a great breed for you. They are the perfect multi-use small flock breed. You can generally count on them to be friendly, and they are beautiful birds to observe. You can't lose with a breed that is good for companionship, show, eggs and meat. The Buff Orpington is the best all-around choice!

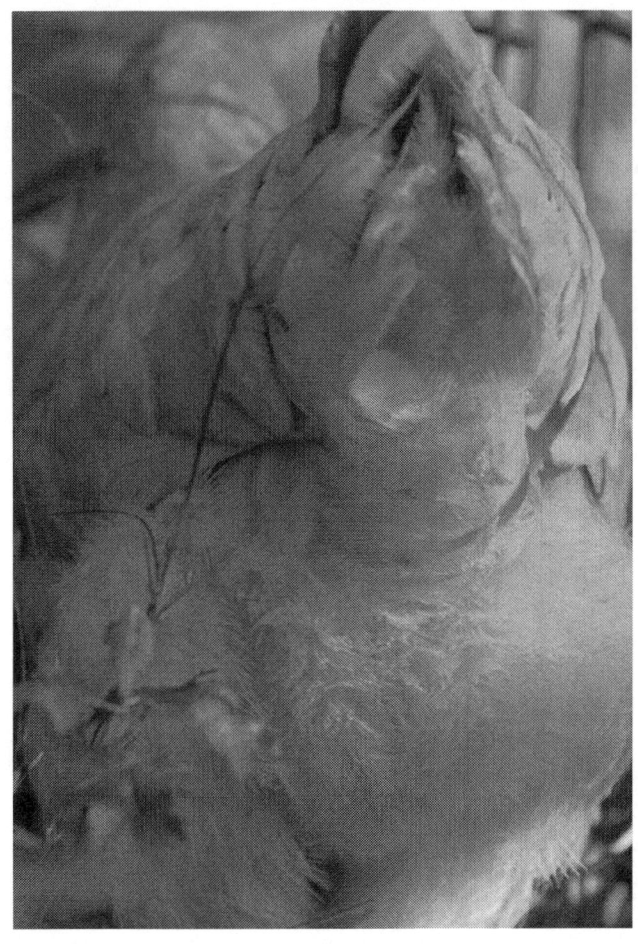

Source: https://www.flickr.com/photos/tenacious_serendipity/3680493946/, Author Haessly Photography

Made in the USA
Monee, IL
07 July 2026